KATIE W

# The
*Creepy Crawly*
# Jokebook

Illustrated by Paul Dowling

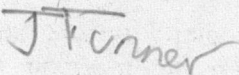

A Magnet Book

# The *Creepy Crawly* **Jokebook**

What do earwigs sing at football matches?
*'Earwigo, earwigo, earwigo . . .'*

What is brown one minute and white the next?
*A rat in a deep freeze.*

What do you call the Incredible Hulk with B.O.?
*The great smell of Brut . . .*

What does an octopus wear?
*A coat of arms.*

To Tim and Roy
— there are no flies on them

First published as a Magnet paperback original 1988
by Methuen Children's Books
A Division of OPG Services Ltd
Michelin House, 81 Fulham Road, London SW3 6RB
Text copyright © 1988 Katie Wales
Illustrations copyright © 1988 Paul Dowling
Printed and bound in Great Britain
by Cox & Wyman Ltd, Reading

Wales, Katie
 The creepy crawly jokebook
 I. Title  II. Dowling, Paul
 828'.91402

ISBN 0-416-13372-X

This paperback is sold subject to the condition
that it shall not, by way of trade or otherwise,
be lent, resold, hired out, or otherwise circulated
without the publisher's prior consent in any form
of binding or cover other than that in which
it is published and without a similar condition
including this condition being imposed
on the subsequent purchaser.

**What has a purple-spotted body, ten hairy legs and eyes on stalks?**
I don't know.
**Nor do I, but there's one creeping up your back . . .**

**Knock, knock.**
Who's there?
**Thumping.**
Thumping who?
**Thumping green and slimy is creeping up your leg.**

**Knock, knock.**
Who's there?
**Weevil.**
Weevil who?
**Weevil work it out.**

'Doctor, doctor, I keep seeing this
spinning insect.'
'Don't worry, it's just a bug that's
going round.'

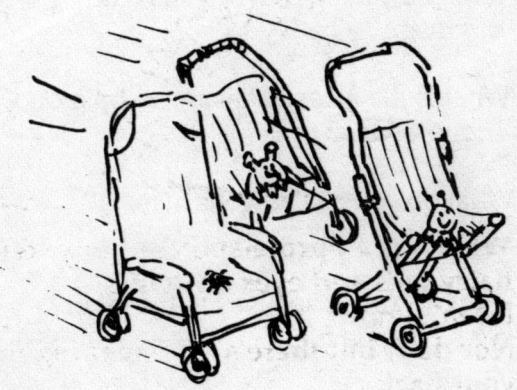

**When insects take a trip, how do they travel?**
They go for a buggy ride.

Why was the insect kicked out of the park?
*It was a litterbug.*

What do you call musical insects?
*Humbugs.*

What is the insect's favourite pop group?
*The Beetles.*

What do you call nervous insects?
*Jitterbugs.*

What did one insect say to the other?
*'Stop bugging me.'*

'Waiter, waiter, what's this in my soup?'
*'I don't know, I can't tell one bug from another.'*

'Waiter, waiter, what's this insect doing in my soup?'
*'I think it's drowning, sir.'*

What did one stick insect say to its friend?
*'Stick around.'*

What makes the letter T so important to a stick insect?
*Without it, it would be a sick insect.*

What kind of insects live on the moon?
*Lunar ticks (lunatics).*

**What's the difference between head lice and nits?**
Head lice crunch more, when you eat them.

**What do you get if you cross a louse with a rabbit?**
Bugs Bunny.

**What do you call an insect from Outer Space?**
Bug Rogers.

**What insect runs away from everything?**
Flee (flea).

**Knock, knock.**
Who's there?
**Flea.**
Flea who?
**Flea blind mice.**

'Waiter, waiter, there's a flea in my soup.'
'Tell him to hop it.'

**What do you call a cheerful flea?**
An 'optimist.

Two fleas were sitting on Robinson Crusoe's back. One hopped off, saying *'Cheerio, see you on Friday.'*

**Did you hear about the angry flea?**
It was hopping mad.

How do fleas travel?
*Itch Iking.*

Did you hear about the flea who failed his exams?
*He didn't come up to scratch.*

Two fleas went to the cinema. When they came out, one said to the other *'Shall we walk or take a dog?'*

How do you find out where a flea has bitten you?
*Start from scratch.*

How do you start a flea race?
*Say 'one, two, flea'.*

What do you call a flea that lives in an idiot's ear?
*A space invader.*

What did Wally do to the flea in his ear?
*Shoot it!*

What is the most faithful insect?
*Fleas – once they find friends, they stick to them.*

**What is a grasshopper?**
An insect on a pogo-stick.

What's the difference between a flea-bitten dog and a bored visitor?
*One's going to itch, and the other's itching to go.*

**If a flea and a fly pass each other, what time is it?**
Fly past flea.

**What is the favourite game of insects?**
Cricket.

**What is green and can jump a mile a minute?**
A grasshopper with hiccups.

**What is green and sooty, and whistles and rubs its back legs together?**
Chimney Cricket.

**The definition of a narrow squeak —**
a thin mouse.

**What's grey and squeaky and hangs around in caves?**
Stalagmice.

**What animals need oiling?**
Mice, because they squeak.


**What do you get if you cross an elephant with a mouse?**
Big holes in the skirting board.

**What's strong and grey and furry, and loves sausages?**
Meaty Mouse.

What's the difference between a tiny elephant and a fat mouse?
*About a thousand kilos.*

What is grey, has four legs and a trunk?
*A mouse going on holiday.*

What is brown, has four legs and a trunk?
*A mouse coming back from his holidays.*

What does a 10-stone mouse say?
*'Here, kitty, kitty!'*

Why isn't an elephant small and grey?
*Because if it was, it would be a mouse.*

When should a mouse carry an umbrella?
*When it's raining cats and dogs.*

Who is the president of the rodents?
*Mouse Tse Tung.*

Which mouse was a Roman emperor?
*Julius Cheeser.*

What is the biggest mouse in the world?
*A hippopoto-mouse.*

What did the mouse do when his friend fell in the water?
*Give him mouse-to-mouse resuscitation.*

**Hickory dickory dock,**
**Three mice ran up the clock,**
**The clock struck one,**
And the rest got way with minor injuries.

What is grey and hairy and lives on a man's face?
*A mousetache.*

**How do mice celebrate when they move house?**
With a mouse-warming party.

**What did the mouse say when his friend broke his front teeth?**
'Hard cheese.'

**Who is a mouse's favourite singer?**
Nana Mousekouri.

**What is a mouse's favourite game?**
Hide n' squeak.

**What do mice do in the day-time?**
Mousework.

**What is a mouse's favourite TV programme?**
Miami Mice.

**What goes 'dot, dot, dash, squeak?'**
Mouse Code.

Why did the mice run out of the chemist's?
*Because there was a puss in Boots.*

**What are grey and furry, and squeak when you pour milk over them?**
Mice Krispies.

**Why do mice wear slippers?**
So they can creep around without cats hearing them.

What is white one minute, and brown the next?
*A rat in a microwave oven.*

What is brown one minute and white the next?
*A rat in a deep-freeze.*

# Crawlies

Why do centipedes make such poor footballers?
*It takes them so long to put their boots on, the match is nearly over.*

What has 50 legs, but cannot walk?
*Half a centipede.*

What do you call a guard with 100 legs?
*A sentrypede.*

What do you get if you cross a centipede with a parrot?
*A walkie-talkie.*

What is worse than a crocodile with toothache?
*A centipede with bunions.*

What did one centipede say to another?
*'You've got a lovely pair of legs, pair of legs, pair of legs . . .'*

What has 100 legs and goes in one ear and out the other?
*A centipede in a corn-field.*

**What do you get if you cross a centipede with a chicken?**
Fewer fights over who gets the drumsticks.

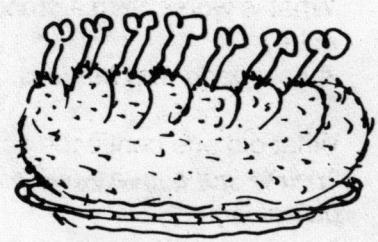

**'Are spiders good to eat?'**
'I shouldn't think so. Why?'

**'There's one crawling out of your sandwich.'**

**What do earwigs sing at football matches?**
'Earwigo, earwigo, earwigo . . .'

**What do you call an Irish spider?**
Paddy-long-legs.

**What would happen if tarantulas were as big as horses?**
If one bit you, you could ride it to hospital.

**What do you get if you cross an elephant with a spider?**
I don't know, but when it crawls over your ceiling, the house will collapse.

**Why are spiders like tops?**
They are always spinning.

**What was the spider doing in the bowl of alphabet soup?**
Learning to read.

**What did Mrs spider say to Mr spider when he broke her new web?**
'Darn it!'

**What does a spider do when it gets angry?**
Go up the wall.

**What pillar doesn't hold a building up?**

A caterpillar.

What does a cat go to sleep on?
*A caterpillar.*

Did you hear about the Irish caterpillar?
*It turned into a frog.*

What does a caterpillar do on New Year's Day?
*Turn over a new leaf.*

What's the definition of a caterpillar?
*A worm in a fur coat.*

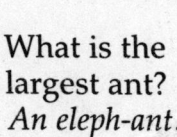

What is the largest ant?
*An eleph-ant.*

Even bigger than that?
*A gi-ant.*

What is smaller than an ant's dinner?
*An ant's mouth.*

How many ants are needed to fill an apartment?
*Ten-ants.*

Why did the elephant put his trunk across the trail?
*To trip up the ants.*

Name a famous scientist ant.
*Albert Antstein.*

**Where do ants eat?**
In a restaur-ant.

**What do you call ant space-travellers?**
Cosmonants.

**What do you call a smart ant?**
Eleg-ant.

**What kind of ants are good at sums?**
Account-ants.

**What kind of ants are very learned?**
Ped-ants.

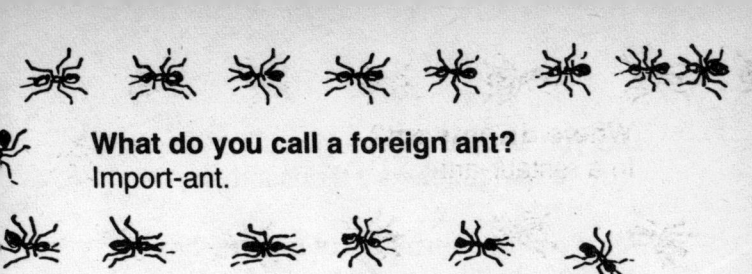

**What do you call a foreign ant?**
Import-ant.

**Where do ants go for their holidays?**
Fr-ants.

**What do you give sick ants?**
Ant-ibiotics.

**What do you call a scruffy, lazy ant?**
Decad-ant.

**What is a termite's favourite breakfast?**
Oak-meal.

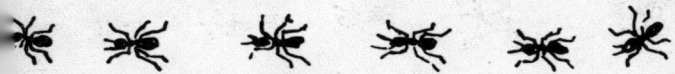

Did you hear about the beautiful Greek termite that lunched a thousand ships?

What did one termite say to the other termite when he saw a house burning?
*'Barbecue tonight!'*

What did the termite say in the pub?
*'Is the bar tender here?'*

Why did the termite eat a sofa and two chairs?
*It had a suite tooth.*

# Buzzers and Stingers

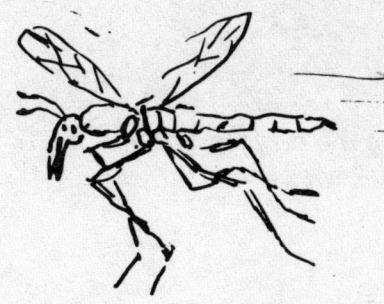

Knock, Knock.
*Who's there?*
Fly.
*Fly who?*
Fly me to the moon . . .


What did the bee say to the flower?
*'Hello, honey.'*


What are the bees' favourite flowers?
*Bee-gonias.*


Who are the cleverest bees?
*Spelling bees.*


What bee is good for your health?
*Vitamin bee.*


**Why do bees hum?**
They don't know the words.

**What goes 'zzub, zzub'?**
A bee flying backwards.

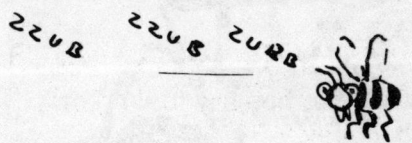

**Why do bees buzz?**
They can't whistle.

**What bee is difficult to hear?**
A mumble bee.

**What do you get if you cross a bee and half a pound of mince?**
Humburgers.

**Who is the bees' favourite painter?**
Pablo Beecasso.

**What is a baby bee?**
A little humbug.

**What is the bees' favourite film?**
'The Sting.'

**Where do bees wait for transport?**
At a buzz-stop.

**What is the bees' favourite composer?**
Bee-thoven.

What goes 'hum-choo, hum-choo'?
*A bee with a cold.*

What is a bee-line?
*The shortest distance between two buzz-stops.*

What did the mother bee say to the little bee?
*'Just beehive yourself, when I comb your hair.'*

Who wrote books for little bees?
*Bee-trix Potter.*

What has brown and yellow stripes, and buzzes along at the bottom of the sea?
*A bee in a submarine.*

What do bees say in summer?
*'Swarm.'*


What did the spider say to the bee?
*'Your honey or your life.'*

Where do bees keep their money?
*In a honey-box.*


Why do bees have sticky hair?
*They have honey-combs.*


What is the bees' favourite TV channel?
*The Bee Bee C.*

**What is the bees' favourite novel?**
The Great Gats-bee.

**Who are the bees' favourite pop-singers?**
The Bee Gees.

**What do you get if you cross a bee with a door-bell?**
A hum-dinger.

**If bees make honey, what do wasps make?**
Waspberry jam.

**Where do you take a sick wasp?**
To waspital.

**What is the wasps' favourite song?**
'A Spoonful of Sugar'.

**What kind of gum do bees chew?**
Bumble-gum.

**Where do wasps go for their holidays?**
Stingapore.

**What do you call a space insect?**
An astro-gnat.

**What insect has a good memory?**
A forget-me-gnat.

**Knock, knock.**
Who's there?
**Amos.**
Amos who?
**Amos quito.**

Knock, knock.
*Who's there?*
Anna.
*Anna who?*
Another mosquito.

What is small and grey, sucks blood, and eats cheese?
*A mouse-quito.*

Why did the mosquito go to the dentist?
*To improve his bite.*

What wears a black cape, flies through the night, and bites?
*A mosquito in a black cape.*

What has six legs, bites, and talks in code?
*A morse-quito.*

Why are mosquitoes religious?
*They prey on you.*

Why are mosquitoes annoying?
*Because they get under your skin.*

What do you get if you cross a mosquito with a knight?
*A bite in shining armour.*

What did one mosquito say to another when they came out of the cinema?
*'Fancy a bite?'*

What has antlers and sucks blood?
*A moose-quito.*

What is a mosquito's favourite sport?
*Skin-diving.*

What do you get if you cross an elephant with some locusts?
*I'm not sure, but if they ever swarm – watch out!*

# Flutteries

**What do insects learn at school?**
Mothematics.

**What insect lives on nothing?**
A moth, because it eats holes.

**What do you call a female moth?**
A myth.

**Why did the moth nibble a hole in the carpet?**
It wanted to see the floor show.

**Why was the moth so unpopular?**
It picked holes in everything.

**What comes out of the wardrobe at 100 m.p.h?**
Stirling Moth.

**What likes to spend the summer in a fur coat and the winter in a wool swim-suit?**
A moth.

**What is the biggest moth?**
A mam-moth.

**Why couldn't the butterfly go to the ball?**
It was a moth ball.

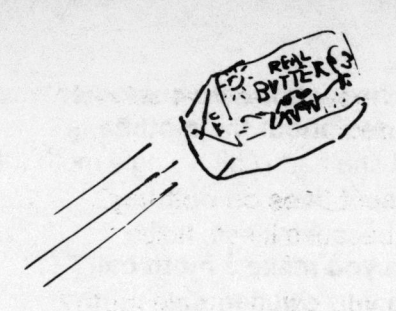

Why did the butterfly?
*Because it saw the milkfloat.*

**Did you hear about the customer who complained about the mothballs?**
She said she hadn't hit a single moth with them.

**How can you make a moth ball?**
Hit it with a fly-swatter.

Where do butterflies hire their dinner jackets?
*Moth Brothers.*

What do you get if you cross a moth with a firefly?
*An insect that can find its way around a dark wardrobe.*

What goes 'snap, crackle, pop'?
*A firefly with a short circuit.*

How do fireflies start a race?
*'Ready, steady, glow.'*

What did one firefly say to another?
*'Got to glow now.'*

What did one bat say to another?
*'Let's hang around together.'*

Why don't bats get kissed much?
*They have bat breath.*

What is a bat's favourite sport?
*Batminton.*

What animal is best at cricket?
*A bat.*

What is the best way to hold a bat?
*By the handle.*

What would you get if you crossed a bat and a magician?
*A flying sorcerer.*

**What do bats do at night?**
Aerobatics.

**What do you get if you cross a bat with a Womble?**
A wombat.

**What is the first thing that bats learn at school?**
The alphabat.

# Wigglies

'Waiter, waiter, there's a maggot in my salad.'
'Well, that's better than half a maggot.'

**What did one maggot say to the other?**
'What's a nice girl like you doing in a joint like this?'

**What's yellow, wiggly and dangerous?**
A maggot with a hand-grenade.

**Who is the worms' Prime Minister?**
Maggot Thatcher.

**Did everything go into the Ark in pairs?**

No, maggots went in apples.

'Waiter, waiter, there's a worm in my soup.'
*'That's not a worm, that's your sausage.'*

What's the maggot army called?
*The apple corps.*

What did one worm say to another when he was late home?
*'Why in earth are you late?'*

How can you tell which end of a worm is its head?
*Tickle its middle, and see which end smiles.*

What's the difference between a worm and a gooseberry?
*Ever tried eating worm pie?*

Did you hear about the man who did bird impressions?
*He ate worms.*

What do you get if you cross a worm with an elephant?
*Big holes in your garden.*

What is the best advice to give a worm?
*Sleep late.*

Why do worms taste like chewing gum?
*Because they're Wrigleys.*

Why did the sparrow fly into the library?
*It was looking for bookworms.*

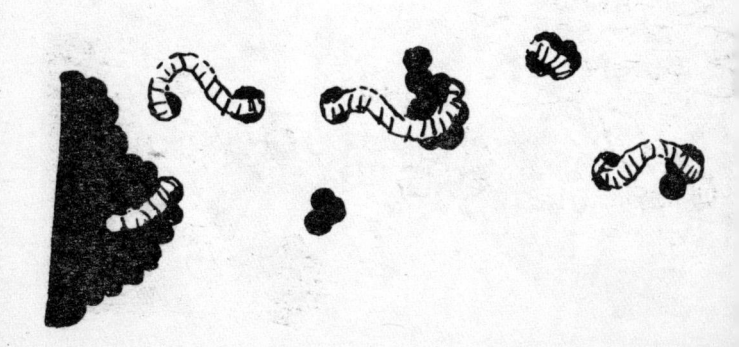

What lives in apples and is an avid reader?
*A bookworm.*

**One woodworm met another. 'How's life?' it asked.**
'Oh, same as usual,' was the reply. 'Boring'.

**Did you hear about Wally woodworm?**
He was found in a brick.

**What makes a glow-worm glow?**
It eats light meals.

What would you do if you found a bookworm chewing your favourite book?
*Take the words right out of its mouth.*

**What did one glow-worm say to the other, when his light went out?**
'Give me a push, my battery is dead.'

**Did you hear about the glow-worm that didn't know if it was coming or glowing?**

**What do you get if you cross a glow-worm with a python?**
A twenty-foot long strip-light that can squeeze you to death.

**What kind of tiles can't you stick on the wall?**
Rep-tiles.

**What's green and wiggly and goes 'Hith, hith'?**
A snake with a lisp.

**What did one snake say to the other?**
'Hiss off!'

**What did the snake get from his admirers?**
Fang mail.

**What is a snake's favourite comedy show?**
Monty Python.

Who is a snake's favourite chat-show host?
*Michael Asp-el.*

Did you hear about the baby snake who asked its mother if they were poisonous. 'Why?' she asked. 'Because I've bitten my tongue!'

Why can't you fool a snake?
*It has no leg to pull.*

Did you hear about the snake who was so frightened, it jumped out of its skin?

What is a python's favourite pop-group?
*The Squeeze.*

What perfume do lady snakes like to wear?
*'Poison', by Dior.*

What do snakes have on their bath-towels?
*Hiss and Hers.*

What do you call a snake who works for the government?
*A civil serpent.*

What do you call a snake that helps the police?
*A grass-snake.*

What did the python say to the viper?
*'I've got a crush on you.'*

**What is a snake's favourite game?**
Snakes and ladders.

**What song do snakes like to sing?**
'Viva Aspana'.

**Why did the viper viper nose?**
Because the adder adder handkerchief.

**What do you give a sick snake?**
Asp-rin.

**What do baby pythons play with?**
Rattle-snakes.

**What would you get if you crossed a new-born snake with a basket-ball?**
A bouncing baby boa.

**What should you do if you find a snake in your bed?**
Sleep in the wardrobe.

**What is a snake's favourite dance?**
Snake, rattle and roll.

**What do you get if you cross a snake with a pig?**
A boar constrictor.

**What do you get if you cross a python with a saxaphone?**
A snake in the brass.

**What is the snake's favourite opera?**
Wiggeletto.

What do you get if you cross a snake with a builder?
*A boa constructor.*

Why can't you trust snakes?
*They speak with forked tongue.*

What snakes are good at sums?
*Adders.*

What do you get if you cross a snake with a hot dog?
*A fangfurter.*

Knock, knock.
*Who's there?*
Eel.
*Eel who?*
Eel be coming round the mountain ...

'Doctor, doctor, I feel like an electric eel.'
*'That's shocking.'*

Have you heard the joke about the slippery eel?
*You wouldn't grasp it.*

What do you get if you cross an electric eel and a sponge?
*Shock absorbers.*

Who was wet and slippery and invaded England?
*William the Conger.*

What is wet and slippery and likes Latin American music?
*A conga eel.*

What did one octopus say to the other?
*'I wanna hold your hand, hand, hand, hand...'*

**How does an octopus go to war?**
Well-armed.

**Did you hear about the octopus with only five tentacles?**
His trousers fit him like a glove.

**What's wet and wiggly and says how do you do sixteen times?**
Two octopusses shaking hands.

**What's an octopuss?**
An eight-sided cat.

**What is wet and wiggly and quick on the draw?**
Billy the Squid.

**What would you get if you crossed an octopus with a cat?**
An animal with eight legs and nine lives.

**Who snatched a baby octopus and held it to ransom?**
Squidnappers.

**What do you call a neurotic octopus?**
A crazy mixed-up squid.

**What is wet and wiggly and good at sums?**
An octoplus.

Who are wet and wiggly and dance on TV?
*The squids from 'Fame'.*

Why did the farmer cross a chicken with an octopus?
*So all the family could have a leg each.*

What would you get if you crossed an octopus with a cow?
*An animal that milks itself.*

What lives under the sea and carries lots of people?
*An octobus.*

What would you get if you crossed an octopus with a mink?
*A fur coat with too many sleeves.*

What did the octopus give his girl-friend for Christmas?
*Four pairs of gloves.*

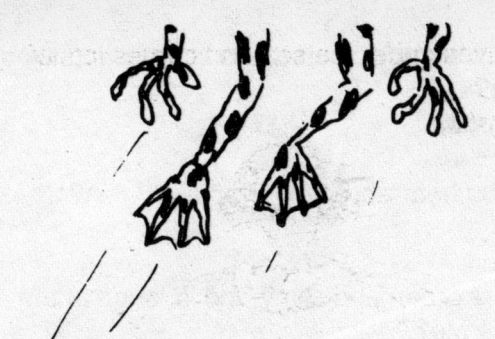

# Slimies
## (and more Hoppers)

What's slimy, coloured and wobbly and lives in the sea?
*A jelly-fish.*

Did you hear about the Wally jelly-fish?
*It set!*

What is green and slimy and is found at the North Pole?
*A lost frog.*

What kind of shoes do frogs like?
*Open toad shoes.*

What do you call a girl with a frog on her head?
*Lily.*

**What is little and green with red spots?**
A frog with measles.

**What do you call a frog spy?**
A croak-and-dagger agent.

**'Waiter, waiter, do you have frogs' legs? Then hop into the kitchen for my soup.'**

**'Waiter, waiter, have you got frogs' legs?'**
'No, sir, I always walk this way.'

**'Waiter, waiter, there's a frog in my soup.'**
'Well, tell him to hop it.'

**What goes 'croak, croak' when it's foggy?**
A frog-horn.

**What do you say to a hitch-hiking frog?**
'Hop in.'

**What is white on the outside and green on the inside?**
A frog sandwich.

**What happens when a frog's car breaks down?**
It gets toad away.

**What do you get if you cross a Muppet with the mist?**
Kermit the fog.

**How do frogs die?**
They Kermit suicide.

Why doesn't Kermit like elephants?
*They always want to play leap-frog with him.*

What is a frog's favourite game?
*Croak-et.*

What is a frog's favourite flower?
*The croakus.*

Where do frogs sit?
*On toadstools.*

What do you get if you cross a frog
with a dog?
*A croaker spaniel.*

How do frogs cross the road?
*They follow the green cross toad.*

What do you get if you cross a planet
with a toad?
*Star warts.*

What do frogs in Glasgow play?
*Hop Scotch.*

What is a toad's favourite ballet?
*Swamp Lake.*

How do toads fly?
*By hoppercraft.*

**What do toads drink?**
Croaka-cola.

'Doctor, doctor, I keep thinking I'm a snail.'
'Don't worry, we'll soon have you out of your shell.'

**What is the strongest animal?**
A snail, because it carries its house on its back.

**What do you do when two snails have a fight?**
Leave them to slug it out.

**What is a slug?**
A snail with a housing problem.

**What was the snail doing on the M1?**
About one mile a day.

**How do snails get their varnish?**
They use snail varnish.

**Where do you find giant snails?**
On the end of a giant's fingers.

**What petrol do snails prefer?**
Shell.

# Pricklies and Hairies

How do you hug a hedgehog?
*Very carefully.*

What do hedgehogs say when they kiss each other?
*'Ouch!'*

Why did the second hedgehog cross the road?
*To see his squash partner.*

What is worse than an elephant on water-skis?
*A hedgehog in a rubber dinghy.*

What do you get if you cross a hedgehog with a mole?
*Leaky tunnels.*

What do you get if you cross a hedgehog with a goat?
*A kid that's hard to handle.*

What do you get if you cross a hedgehog with a nettle?
*Extremely sore hands.*

What do you get if you cross a hedgehog with a giraffe?
*An eight-foot tall toothbrush.*

What do you get if you cross a hedgehog
with an alarm clock?
*A stickler for punctuality.*

What do hedgehogs eat with cheese?
*Prickled onions.*

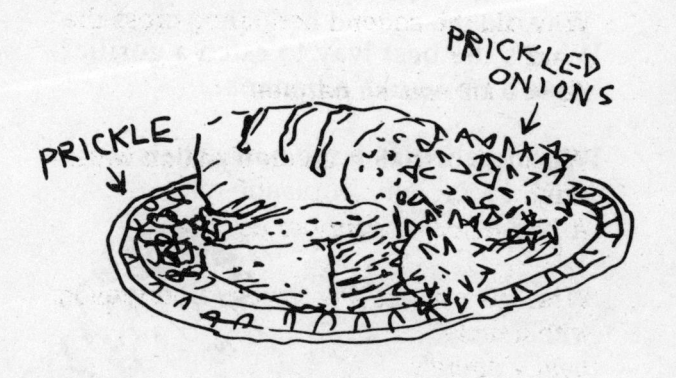

What pine has the largest needles?
*A porcupine.*

**What would you get if you crossed an elephant with a cactus?**
The biggest porcupine in the world.

**What's the difference between a coyote and a flea?**
One howls on the prairie, and the other prowls on the hairy.

**Why are gorillas big and hairy?**
So you can tell them apart from gooseberries.

**What's the difference between a gorilla and a Wally?**
You can talk to a gorilla.

**What's the best way to catch a gorilla?**
Make a noise like a banana.

**Why do gorillas have hairy coats?**
They'd look silly in plastic macs.

**What do you do if you want toast in the jungle?**
Put some bread under the gorilla.

**How did the gorilla escape from its cage?**
With a monkey wrench.

**How do you address a gorilla?**
Very politely.

**Where does a two-ton gorilla sleep?**
Anywhere it wants to.

**What do you call a gorilla that works with cars?**
A grease monkey.

What did the monkey say when it fell out of the tree?
*AAARRGGHH!!!!*

What do monkeys sing at Christmas?
*'Jungle bells, jungle bells.'*

What do you get if you cross a monkey with a flower?
*A chimp-pansy.*

**Where do baby monkeys sleep?**
*Ape-ricots.*

**What monkeys are white and fluffy?**
*Meringue-utans.*

**What monkeys are Irish?**
*O'rang-utans.*

**Who was a famous general of the apes?**
*Napoleon Baboonaparte.*

**What happened when King Kong swallowed Big Ben?**
*He found it time-consuming.*

Why did King Kong join the army?
*He wanted to learn about gorilla warfare.*

What do you get if you cross King Kong with a frog?
*A gorilla that catches aeroplanes with its tongue.*

What business is King Kong in?
*Monkey business.*

**What is brown and hairy and runs through the desert?**
A camel train.

**How do you hire a camel?**
Put a brick under each foot.

**What is brown and hairy, and has three humps?**
A camel with a rucksack.

**What do camels carry when it rains?**
Humpbrellas.

**What do you get if you cross a camel with a cow?**
Lumpy milkshakes.

**What is light brown and hairy, has two humps and a trunk?**
A camel going on holiday.

**What do you get if you cross a camel with a rose?**
A flower that never needs watering.

**Who is a camel's favourite singer?**
Englebert Hump-erdink.

**Why was the camel unhappy?**
Because it had the hump.

**What is brown, hairy and dangerous and lives in Tibet?**
Yak the Ripper.

**What do you get if you cross an elephant with the Abominable Snowman?**
A jumbo yeti.

**What do you get if you cross a yeti with a kangaroo?**
A fur coat with big pockets.

# Smellies

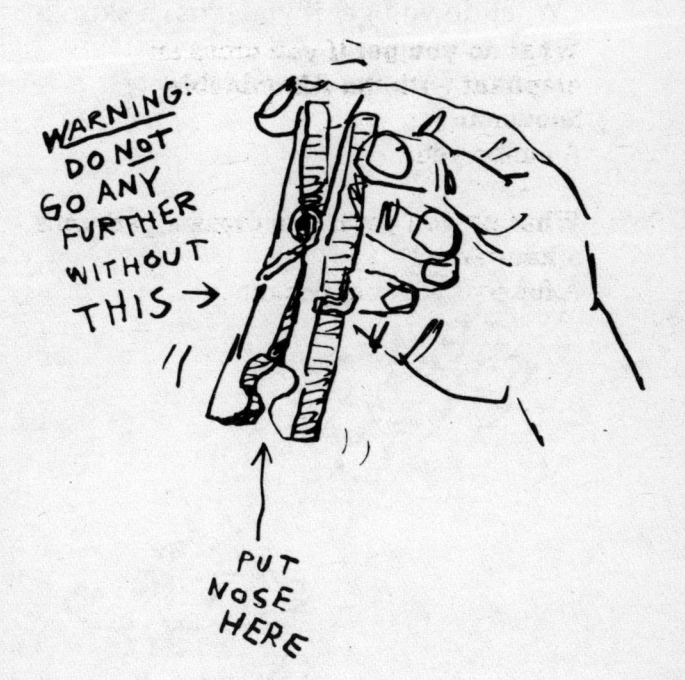

WARNING: DO NOT GO ANY FURTHER WITHOUT THIS →

PUT NOSE HERE

Did you hear the joke about the skunk?
*Never mind, it stinks.*

What do you call a dead skunk?
*Ex-stinked.*

What do you get if you cross a skunk
with a boomerang?
*A terrible smell you can't get rid of.*

Who's the smelliest hairiest monarch in the world?
*King Pong.*

What's black and white and red all over?
*A skunk with nappy rash.*

What do you get if you cross a skunk
with a hedgehog?
*A porcupong.*

What do you get if you cross a skunk
with a gorilla?
*I don't know, but it wouldn't have much
trouble finding a seat on the bus!*

What do you get if you cross a skunk
with an astronaut?
*An animal that stinks to high heaven.*

What do you get if you cross a skunk
with a tiger?
*An animal that gasses you before it eats you.*

What do you get if you cross a skunk
with an owl?
*A bird that smells and doesn't give a hoot.*

What do you get if you cross a skunk
with a hedgehog?
*A smelly pincushion.*

What do you get if you cross a skunk with a bear?
*Winnie the Pooh.*

**What did the skunk say when the wind changed direction?**
'It's all coming back to me now.'

**How do you keep a skunk from smelling?**
Hold its nose.

**How many skunks does it take to make a big stink?**
A phew.

**Why was the skunk grumpy?**
Because it had a stinking headache.

**Why do pigs argue so much?**
They like to make a stink.

**What did one philosophical pig say to the other?**
'I stink therefore I am.'

**What's pink and smells?**
A pig's snout.

**What smells worse than a pig in a sty?**
Two pigs in a sty.

**Which town do pigs like the least?**
Bath.

**What is pink and smelly and can't stand still?**
A pig in a tumble dryer.

What is pink and smelly and plays football?
*Queen's Pork Rangers.*

Who was the cleverest pig scientist in the world?
*Albert Einswine.*

What is a pig's favourite play?
*Hamlet.*

What is a pig's favourite novel?
*The Pigwick Papers.*

What do you give a sick pig?
*Oinkment.*

How do you take a sick pig to hospital?
*By hambulance.*

What did one pig say to the other?
*'Let's be pen pals.'*

What do you get if you cross a pig with a telephone?
*Crackling on the line.*

What do you get if you cross a pig with a zebra?
*Striped sausages.*

What do you get if you cross a pig with an elephant?
*Extra large pork chops.*

What do you get if you cross a pig with a drummer?
*Ham rolls.*

**What do you get if you cross a pig with a flea?**
Pork scratchings.

**What do you call a pig who tells dreary jokes?**
A big boar.

**Where do American pigs live?**
In styscrapers.

**Why did the three little pigs leave home?**
Their father was a boar.

**Why did the little pig eat so much?**
He was making a hog of himself.

**What do you call a pig with no clothes on?**
Streaky bacon.

**What do you call a pig thief?**
A hamburglar.

**Where do hogs keep their money?**
In piggy banks.

**What kind of pigs do you find on the M1?**
Road hogs.